HEALTHY FAMILY FOOD

70 fabulous recipes

MARKS &
SPENCER

PLEASE NOTE that the cup and spoon
measurements used in this book are metric.
A conversion chart appears on page 126.

Marks and Spencer plc and ACP Publishing Pty
Limited hereby exclude all liability to the extent
permitted by law for any errors or omissions in this
book and for any loss, damage or expense (whether
direct or indirect) suffered by a third party relying
on any information contained in this book.

This edition first published in 2006 by
ACP Publishing Pty Limited.
Exclusively for Marks and Spencer p.l.c.

www.marksandspencer.com

Copyright ACP Publishing Pty Limited 2006

ISBN: 1-90377705-4

Printed and bound in China

contents

minted tomato, rhubarb and lime frappé

MAKES 1.25 LITRES (5 CUPS)
PER 250ML 0.4G FAT;
80 CALORIES (334KJ)

4 cups (440g) chopped rhubarb
$^1/_4$ cup (55g) sugar
$^1/_4$ cup (60ml) water
4 medium tomatoes (760g), peeled, seeded, chopped
2$^1/_4$ tablespoons lime juice
3 cups ice cubes
2 tablespoons chopped fresh mint

1 Combine rhubarb, sugar and the water in medium saucepan; simmer, covered, about 10 minutes or until rhubarb is tender. Cool.
2 Blend or process rhubarb mixture with remaining ingredients until smooth; serve immediately.

drinks

papaya, strawberry and orange juice

MAKES 1 LITRE (4 CUPS)
PER 250ML 0.3G FAT; 88 CALORIES (368KJ)

1 large papaya (1.2kg), chopped coarsely
250g strawberries
3/4 cup (180ml) fresh orange juice

1 Blend papaya, strawberries and orange juice together until smooth.

TIPS refrigerate all ingredients before making the juice. Serve the juice within 30 minutes of making.

orange, carrot and ginger juice

MAKES 1 CUP (250ML)
PER 250ML 0.3G FAT; 105 CALORIES (439KJ)

1 large orange (300g), peeled, chopped coarsely
1 small carrot (70g), halved lengthways
2cm piece fresh ginger (10g)

1 Push orange, carrot and ginger through juice extractor. Stir to combine.

TIPS refrigerate all ingredients before making the juice. Serve the juice within 30 minutes of making.

banana passionfruit soy smoothie

MAKES 1 LITRE (4 CUPS)
PER 250ML 4.7G FAT; 157 CALORIES (656KJ)

You need about six passionfruit for this recipe.

$^1/_2$ cup (125ml) passionfruit pulp
2 cups (500ml) soy milk
2 medium ripe bananas (400g), chopped coarsely

1 Strain passionfruit pulp through sieve into small bowl; reserve liquid and seeds.
2 Blend passionfruit liquid, milk and banana, in batches, until smooth.
3 Pour smoothie into large jug; stir in reserved seeds.

mixed berry smoothie

MAKES 1 LITRE (4 CUPS)
PER 250ML 3.6G FAT; 192 CALORIES (803KJ)

250ml frozen low-fat strawberry yogurt, softened slightly
$1^1/_3$ cups (200g) frozen mixed berries
3 cups (750ml) skimmed milk

1 Blend ingredients, in batches, until smooth.
2 Serve immediately.

drinks

pineapple orange frappé

MAKES 1 LITRE (4 CUPS)
PER 250ML 0.2G FAT; 74 CALORIES (309KJ)

1 medium pineapple (1.25kg), chopped coarsely
$^1/_2$ cup (125ml) orange juice
3 cups crushed ice
1 tablespoon finely grated orange rind

1 Blend pineapple and juice, in batches, until smooth.
2 Pour into large jug with crushed ice and rind; stir to combine.
Serve immediately.

coconut mango thickshake

SERVES 6
PER SERVING 14.1G FAT; 274 CALORIES (1145KJ)

3 medium mangoes (1.3kg)
200ml can coconut milk
$1^1/_2$ cups (375ml) milk
500ml vanilla ice-cream, chopped

1 Cut mango flesh from both sides of the seed. Remove the skin
and freeze mango for several hours or until firm.
2 Blend milks, mango and ice-cream, in two batches, until smooth.
Serve immediately.

TIP for a reduced-fat version of the thickshake, substitute light
coconut milk, no-fat milk and low-fat ice-cream.
You can also use peaches, nectarines, plums, apricots, bananas or
berries, or a combination if you prefer, instead of the mango.

sweet saffron lassi

MAKES 3 CUPS (750ML)
PER 250ML 6.4G FAT; 187 CALORIES (782KJ)

*Lassis are yogurt-based drinks which
are an excellent cooling foil for a fiery
Indian curry.*

pinch saffron threads
1 tablespoon boiling water
2 cups (560g) plain yogurt
1 cup (250ml) iced water
2 tablespoons caster sugar
$1/2$ teaspoon ground cardamom
ice cubes

1 Combine saffron and the boiling water
in small heatproof cup; stand 5 minutes.
2 Whisk yogurt, the iced water, sugar
and cardamom in large jug; stir in saffron
mixture.
3 Serve lassi over ice cubes.

drinks

9

iced mocha

SERVES 2
PER SERVING 43.9G FAT;
645 CALORIES (2696KJ)

1 tablespoon instant coffee powder
1 tablespoon boiling water
2 tablespoons chocolate-flavoured
topping
1$\frac{1}{2}$ cups (375ml) cold milk
4 scoops (500ml) vanilla ice-cream
$\frac{1}{2}$ cup (125ml) cream, whipped
1 teaspoon drinking chocolate

1 Combine coffee and the water in large
heatproof jug, stir until dissolved.
2 Stir in chocolate-flavoured topping and
milk. Pour into two large glasses and top
each with 2 scoops vanilla ice-cream and
cream, then sprinkle with sifted drinking
chocolate; serve immediately.

drinks

10

spiced iced coffee milkshake

MAKES 1 LITRE (4 CUPS)
PER 250ML 3G FAT; 153 CALORIES (640KJ)

1/4 cup (20g) ground espresso coffee
3/4 cup (180ml) boiling water
2 cardamom pods, bruised
1/4 teaspoon ground cinnamon
1 tablespoon brown sugar
3 scoops (375ml) low-fat vanilla
ice-cream
2 1/2 cups (625ml) skimmed milk

1 Place coffee then the water in coffee
plunger; stand 2 minutes before plunging.
Pour coffee into small heatproof bowl with
cardamom, cinnamon and sugar; stir to
dissolve sugar then cool 10 minutes.
2 Strain coffee mixture through fine sieve
into blender or processor; process with
ice-cream and milk until smooth. Serve
immediately.

drinks

11

spiced chocolate milk

SERVES 2
PER SERVING 14.1G FAT;
244 CALORIES (1020KJ)

30g dark eating chocolate, melted
2 cups (500ml) milk
1 cinnamon stick

1 Using a teaspoon, drizzle melted chocolate onto the insides of heatproof glasses.
2 Combine milk and cinnamon stick in medium saucepan, stir over low heat until heated through, but not boiling. Remove cinnamon. Pour milk into glasses.

drinks

vanilla cafe latte

SERVES 2
PER SERVING 9.9G FAT
183 CALORIES (765KJ)

$^1/_3$ cup (30g) coarsely ground coffee beans
500ml (2 cups) milk
1 teaspoon vanilla extract

1 Combine ingredients in medium saucepan, stir, over low heat until heated through, but not boiling.
2 Pour through fine strainer into heatproof serving glasses.

real hot chocolate

SERVES 6
PER SERVING 35.3G FAT;
557 CALORIES (2328KJ)

1 litre (4 cups) milk
200g milk eating chocolate, chopped
100g dark eating chocolate, chopped
$^3/_4$ cup (180ml) thickened cream
1 tablespoon Tia Maria or Baileys
Irish Cream liqueur
90g Maltesers, chopped

1 Combine milk and both chocolates in
medium saucepan; stir over low heat until
chocolate is melted. Do not boil milk.
2 Beat cream and liqueur in small bowl
of electric mixer until soft peaks form.
3 Divide milk among heatproof serving
glasses, top with cream mixture and
sprinkle with Maltesers.

drinks

toasted muesli

SERVES 2
PREPARATION TIME 15 MINUTES
COOKING TIME 45 MINUTES
(PLUS COOLING TIME)
PER SERVING 4.4G FAT;
342 CALORIES (1433KJ)

1 cup rolled oats (90g)
^{1}/4 cup (15g) unprocessed bran
^{1}/4 cup (35g) finely chopped dried apricots
^{1}/4 cup (20g) finely chopped dried apples
2 tablespoons sultanas
1 tablespoon honey
1 tablespoon water
1 cup (250ml) skimmed milk

1 Combine oats, bran and fruit in medium bowl; stir in combined honey and water.
2 Spread mixture onto oven tray; bake in slow oven for about 45 minutes or until toasted, stirring occasionally. Cool.
3 Serve muesli with milk, and fresh fruit, if desired.

STORE muesli can be refrigerated in an airtight container for several weeks.

blueberry muffins

MAKES 12 MUFFINS
PREPARATION TIME 10 MINUTES
COOKING TIME 20 MINUTES
PER MUFFIN 0.5G FAT;
130 CALORIES (545KJ)

cooking-oil spray
1 cup (150g) white self-raising flour
1 cup (160g) wholemeal self-raising flour
^{1}/2 cup (100g) firmly packed brown sugar
1 cup (150g) fresh or frozen blueberries
2 egg-whites, beaten lightly
^{1}/3 cup (80ml) prepared apple sauce
^{3}/4 cup (180ml) skimmed milk

1 Lightly coat a 12-hole muffin pan (^{1}/3-cup capacity) with cooking-oil spray.
2 Sift flours into a large bowl; stir in sugar and blueberries.
3 Stir in egg-whites, sauce and milk until almost combined (do not over-mix); spoon into prepared pan.
4 Cook in a hot oven about 20 minutes or until cooked when tested.

STORE muffins can be made a day ahead and kept in an airtight container at room temperature, or frozen.

rolled barley

rolled rice

rolled rye

rolled triticale

rolled oats

porridge with rolled grains

We used water to make these porridges, but skimmed milk or various fruit juices are an option, if desired. The amounts given below for each type of porridge are enough to make 4 servings.

GRAIN	amount	soaking liquid	cooking liquid	cooking time	makes
ROLLED RICE	³/₄ cup (75g)	1¹/₂ cups (375ml)	³/₄ cup (180ml)	10 minutes	1³/₄ cups per serving 0.5g fat; 238kJ (57 cal); 0g saturated fat; 0.6g fibre; 14.8g carbohydrate
ROLLED BARLEY	³/₄ cup (75g)	1¹/₂ cups (375ml)	³/₄ cup (180ml)	25 minutes	1¹/₂ cups per serving 0.1g fat; 276kJ (66 cal); 0.1g saturated fat; 2.1g fibre; 11.5g carbohydrate
ROLLED OATS	³/₄ cup (60g)	1¹/₂ cups (375ml)	¹/₂ cup (125ml)	10 minutes	1¹/₂ cups per serving 1.3g fat; 233kJ (56 cal); 0.2g saturated fat; 1g fibre; 9.3g carbohydrate
ROLLED RYE	³/₄ cup (75g)	1¹/₂ cups (375ml)	1¹/₂ cups (375ml)	50 minutes	1³/₄ cups per serving 0.5g fat; 248kJ (59 cal); 2.3g fibre; 12.1g carbohydrate
ROLLED TRITICALE*	³/₄ cup (75g)	1¹/₂ cups (375ml)	1¹/₂ cups (375ml)	45 minutes	1¹/₄ cups per serving 0.5g fat; 244kJ (58 cal); 11.7g carbohydrate

1 Place grain and soaking liquid in medium bowl, cover; stand at room temperature overnight.
2 Place undrained grain in medium saucepan; cook, stirring, until mixture comes to a boil. Add cooking liquid, reduce heat; simmer, uncovered, for required cooking time. Serve warm with toppings of your choice.

Triticale is a rye/wheat hybrid grain available in health stores.

TOPPINGS

These toppings are enough for a single serving of porridge.

¹/₂ cup (125ml) skimmed milk	0.1G FAT; 45 CAL (189KJ); 0.1G SATURATED FAT; 0G FIBRE; 6.5G CARB.
1 teaspoon honey	0G FAT; 23 CAL (94KJ); 0G SATURATED FAT; 0G FIBRE; 22.2G CARB.
1 tablespoon low-fat vanilla yogurt	0G FAT; 16 CAL (68KJ); 0G SATURATED FAT; 0G FIBRE; 2.4G CARB.
pinch cinnamon	0G FAT; 2 CAL (6KJ)
¹/₂ mashed banana	0.1G FAT; 57 CAL (240KJ); 0G SATURATED FAT; 5.1G FIBRE; 45.8G CARB.
1 tablespoon dried fruit	0.1G FAT; 37 CAL (156KJ); 0.1G SATURATED FAT; 1.1G FIBRE; 13G CARB.
2 teaspoons toasted shredded coconut	2G FAT; 19 CAL (79KJ); 1.7G SATURATED FAT; 0.4G FIBRE; 0.2G CARB.

breakfasts

citrus compote

Pink or ruby grapefruit have coral-pink flesh and a shell-pink blush to their skin, and are sweeter than the yellow-skinned variety.

SERVES 4
PREPARATION TIME 20 MINUTES
(PLUS STANDING TIME)
PER SERVING 0.7G FAT;
164 CALORIES (685KJ)

2 large limes (160g)
3 large oranges (900g)
2 medium pink grapefruit (850g)
2 teaspoons sugar
$^1/_2$ vanilla pod, split
1 tablespoon small fresh mint leaves

1 Grate the rind of 1 lime and 1 orange finely; reserve grated rind. Peel remaining lime, remaining oranges, and grapefruit.
2 Segment all citrus over a large bowl to save juice, removing and discarding membrane from each segment. Add segments to bowl with sugar, vanilla pod and reserved rind; stir gently to combine.
3 Stand, covered, at room temperature 5 minutes; sprinkle with mint leaves.

strawberry hotcakes with blueberry sauce

With a juicy centre and sweet taste, blueberries have easily become one of our year-round all-time-favourite berries.

SERVES 4
PREPARATION TIME 15 MINUTES
COOKING TIME 20 MINUTES
PER SERVING 3.4G FAT;
391 CALORIES (1639KJ)

1 egg, separated
2 egg whites, extra
$1/2$ cup (125ml) apple sauce
1 teaspoon vanilla essence
2 cups (560g) low-fat plain yogurt
$1^3/4$ cups (280g) wholemeal self-raising flour
250g strawberries, hulled and chopped coarsely

BLUEBERRY SAUCE

150g blueberries, chopped coarsely
2 tablespoons sugar
1 tablespoon water

1 Using electric mixer, beat all egg whites in small bowl until soft peaks form.
2 Meanwhile, combine egg yolk, apple sauce, essence, yogurt, flour and strawberries in large bowl; fold in egg whites.
3 Pour $1/4$ cup batter into heated large lightly greased non-stick frying pan; using spatula, spread batter to shape into a round. Cook, over low heat, about 2 minutes or until bubbles appear on the surface. Turn hotcake; cook until lightly browned on other side. Remove from pan; cover to keep warm. Repeat with remaining batter. Serve with blueberry sauce.

BLUEBERRY SAUCE combine ingredients in small saucepan; bring to a boil, stirring constantly. Reduce heat; simmer 2 minutes. Remove from heat; cool. Blend or process blueberry mixture until smooth.

roast garlic mushrooms with crispy ham

200g button mushrooms
150g flat mushrooms, halved
100g brown mushrooms
1 medium red onion (170g), sliced thinly
1 clove garlic, crushed
1 tablespoon lemon juice
coarsely ground black pepper
cooking-oil spray
200g wafer-thin lean ham
1/2 small French stick, sliced thickly
8 basil leaves, torn

SERVES 2
PREPARATION TIME 10 MINUTES
COOKING TIME 25 MINUTES
PER SERVING 5.2G FAT; 263 CALORIES (1103KJ)

1 Combine mushrooms, onion, garlic, lemon juice and pepper in baking dish; spray lightly with cooking-oil spray. Cook in hot oven, uncovered, about 20 minutes or until mushrooms are tender, stirring occasionally.

2 Meanwhile, spread ham on oven tray; cook in hot oven, about 15 minutes or until crisp.

3 Toast bread on both sides; stir basil through mushroom mixture. Serve bread topped with ham and mushroom.

STORE cook recipe just before serving.

corned beef hash with poached eggs

1 medium brown onion (150g),
chopped finely
3 medium potatoes (600g),
grated coarsely
500g cooked corned beef, shredded
2 tablespoons finely chopped fresh
flat-leaf parsley
2 tablespoons plain flour
2 eggs, beaten lightly
1 tablespoon vegetable oil
4 eggs, extra
1 tablespoon shredded fresh basil

SERVES 2
PREPARATION TIME 20 MINUTES
PER SERVING 37.8G FAT; 809 CALORIES (3387KJ)

1 Combine onion, potato, beef, parsley, flour and egg in large bowl.
Using hands, shape mixture into four patties.
2 Heat oil in large non-stick frying pan; cook patties until browned
both sides and cooked through.
3 Break extra eggs into greased egg rings in barely simmering water;
poach eggs until cooked as desired. Carefully lift rings away from
eggs; lift eggs from water, drain.
4 Serve hash patties topped with poached eggs; top with basil.

breakfasts

25

mini spinach frittata

SERVES 2
PREPARATION TIME 10 MINUTES
COOKING TIME 20 MINUTES
PER SERVING 0.8G FAT;
46 CALORIES (194KJ)

250g baby spinach leaves
$1/2$ teaspoon olive oil
1 small brown onion (80g), sliced thinly
1 tablespoon water
pinch ground nutmeg
2 egg whites
2 tablespoons skimmed milk
$1/2$ teaspoon olive oil, extra

1 Steam or microwave spinach until tender. Drain; chop roughly.
2 Heat oil in medium non-stick saucepan; cook onion and the water. Cover; cook until onion is soft. Combine spinach, onion mixture, nutmeg, egg whites and milk in bowl.
3 Lightly grease four egg rings with a little of the extra oil; heat remaining extra oil in large non-stick frying pan. Place egg rings in pan; fill with egg mixture.
4 Cook until mixture is set; remove egg rings. Turn frittata; cook frittata until lightly browned underneath. Serve with a green salad, if desired.

STORE cook recipe just before serving.

bacon, cheese and chilli muffins

MAKES 18
PREPARATION TIME 10 MINUTES
COOKING TIME 30 MINUTES
PER MUFFIN FAT 10.2G;
200 CALORIES (836KJ)

8 bacon rashers (560g), rind removed, chopped coarsely
2^1/$_2$ cups (375g) self-raising flour
80g butter, chopped
1 teaspoon sweet paprika
^{1}/$_2$ teaspoon dried chilli flakes
1^1/$_2$ cups (180g) coarsely grated cheddar cheese
310g can sweetcorn, drained
1 egg
1 cup (250ml) buttermilk

1 Preheat oven to moderately hot (200°C/180°C fan-assisted). Oil three 6-hole (^{1}/$_3$-cup/180ml) muffin pans.
2 Cook bacon in heated medium frying pan, stirring, until crisp; drain on absorbent paper.
3 Process flour, butter, paprika and chilli until mixture resembles breadcrumbs. Transfer to medium bowl; stir in bacon, cheese, corn and combined egg and buttermilk.
4 Spoon ^{1}/$_4$ cup of the mixture into each prepared hole; bake, uncovered, for about 20 minutes. Turn muffins onto wire rack; serve warm.

TIP these muffins are best made using a strong vintage cheddar.

maple rice pudding with pecans and dates

SERVES 8
PREPARATION TIME 10 MINUTES
COOKING TIME 40 MINUTES
PER SERVING FAT 41.1G;
579 CALORIES (2420KJ)

1^1/$_2$ litres (6 cups) milk
2 cups (500ml) cream
^{2}/$_3$ cup (160ml) maple syrup
^{1}/$_4$ teaspoon ground cinnamon
^{2}/$_3$ cup (130g) medium-grain white rice
^{1}/$_2$ cup (85g) coarsely chopped seeded dates
^{1}/$_2$ cup (70g) toasted pecans, chopped coarsely

1 Combine milk, cream, syrup and cinnamon in large saucepan; bring to a boil, stirring occasionally.
2 Gradually stir in rice; cook, uncovered, over low heat, stirring occasionally, about 40 minutes or until rice is tender.
3 Serve rice pudding with combined dates and nuts; drizzle with a little more maple syrup, if desired.

breakfasts

breakfast with the lot

Plum tomatoes, also known as roma or Italian tomatoes, are small and oval in shape; they are often used in Italian dishes.

SERVES 4
PREPARATION TIME 10 MINUTES
COOKING TIME 25 MINUTES
PER SERVING 7G FAT;
160 CALORIES (680KJ)

2 large plum tomatoes (180g), quartered
4 eggs
4 slices multigrain bread
60g lean ham
50g baby spinach leaves

1 Preheat oven to hot. Line oven tray with baking paper.
2 Place tomato, cut-side up, on prepared tray; roast, uncovered, in hot oven about 25 minutes or until softened and lightly browned.
3 Meanwhile, place enough water in a large shallow non-stick frying pan to come halfway up the side; bring to a boil. Break eggs, one at a time, into small bowl, sliding each into pan; allow water to return to a boil. Cover pan, turn off heat; stand about 4 minutes or until a light film of egg white has set over each yolk.
4 Toast bread slices until lightly browned both sides.
5 Using an egg slide, remove eggs, one at a time, from pan; place egg, still on slide, on absorbent-paper-lined saucer to blot up any poaching liquid. Serve toast topped with ham, spinach, egg then tomato.

chocolate hazelnut croissants

MAKES 8
PREPARATION TIME 15 MINUTES
COOKING TIME 15 MINUTES
PER CROISSANT 17.7G FAT;
275 CALORIES (1153KJ)

2 sheets ready-rolled puff pastry
$^1/_3$ cup (110g) Nutella
30g dark chocolate, grated finely
25g butter, melted
1 tablespoon icing sugar mixture

1 Preheat oven to hot. Lightly grease two oven trays.
2 Cut pastry sheets diagonally to make four triangles. Spread Nutella over triangles, leaving a 1cm border; sprinkle each evenly with chocolate.
3 Roll triangles, starting at one wide end; place 3cm apart on prepared trays with the tips tucked under and the ends slightly curved in to form crescent shape. Brush croissants with melted butter.
4 Bake, uncovered, in hot oven about 12 minutes or until croissants are browned lightly and cooked through. Sieve croissants with icing sugar; serve warm or at room temperature.

TOAST OF THE TOWN

Raise your glass in a toast to crusty, delectable bruschetta (pronounced broos-ketta). What could be easier than bread topped with the following flavour combinations? And the praise for these little numbers will be overwhelming.

bruschetta with three toppings

All toppings are enough for one bread stick only, giving 25 servings.

30cm French bread stick
2 cloves garlic, peeled, halved
2 tablespoons olive oil

Trim ends from bread stick, cut bread into 1cm slices. Grill or toast bread both sides until browned lightly. Rub garlic over one side of each piece of toast; brush lightly with oil. Top with desired topping.

courgette and pine nut

PER SERVING 4.2G FAT; 101 CALORIES (421KJ)

2 tablespoons olive oil
1 tablespoon pine nuts
1 clove garlic, crushed
1 baby aubergine (60g), chopped finely
1 small tomato (130g), chopped finely
2 small courgettes (180g), chopped finely
6 pitted black olives, chopped finely
2 tablespoons sultanas
2 teaspoons red wine vinegar
1 tablespoon finely chopped fresh basil
1 tablespoon finely chopped fresh
flat-leaf parsley

Heat oil in medium frying pan; cook nuts, garlic and aubergine, stirring, 5 minutes. Add tomato, courgettes, olives, sultanas and vinegar; cook, stirring, until courgettes are soft, cool. Stir in basil and parsley. Spoon vegetable mixture onto toasts.

roasted red pepper and olive

PER SERVING 2.4G FAT; 86 CALORIES (360KJ)

2 large red peppers (700g)
1 tablespoon lemon juice
2 teaspoons drained capers
1 clove garlic, crushed
1/4 cup finely chopped fresh
flat-leaf parsley
1 teaspoon ground cumin
2 teaspoons sugar
1/3 cup (40g) pitted black olives,
sliced finely

Quarter peppers, remove and discard seeds and membranes. Roast under grill or in very hot oven, skin-side up, until skin blisters and blackens. Cover pepper pieces with plastic or paper for 5 minutes, peel away skin. Blend or process pepper with juice, capers, garlic, parsley, cumin and sugar until smooth. Stir in olives. Spoon pepper mixture onto toasts.

tomato and basil

PER SERVING 2.4G FAT; 40 CALORIES (167KJ)

3 small tomatoes (390g), deseeded and chopped finely
1 small red onion (100g), chopped finely
1/4 cup finely shredded fresh basil
1 tablespoon olive oil

Combine ingredients in small bowl; spoon tomato mixture onto toasts. Top with small fresh basil leaves, if desired.

DIPS

Avoid the temptation to snack on junk food high in saturated fat by keeping a supply of bagel chips and healthy dips on hand. Serve them to guests too – they'll never know they're eating low-fat!

spicy tomato salsa

SERVES 4
PREPARATION TIME 10 MINUTES
COOKING TIME 15 MINUTES
(PLUS COOLING TIME)
PER SERVING 0.4G FAT;
37 CALORIES (153KJ)

4 medium tomatoes (760g),
chopped finely
2 cloves garlic, crushed
1 small brown onion (80g),
sliced thinly
1 teaspoon Cajun seasoning
2 teaspoons no-added-salt
tomato paste

Combine tomatoes with remaining ingredients in small saucepan. Cook, stirring, about 15 minutes or until onion is soft and sauce has thickened; cool.

STORE salsa can be made 3 days ahead and refrigerated, covered.

baba ghanoush

SERVES 4
PREPARATION TIME 10 MINUTES
(PLUS REFRIGERATION TIME)
COOKING TIME 35 MINUTES
(PLUS COOLING TIME)
PER SERVING 2.2G FAT;
52 CALORIES (218KJ)

2 small aubergines (460g)
$1/3$ cup (80ml) low-fat plain yogurt
1 tablespoon lemon juice
2 cloves garlic, crushed
1 teaspoon tahini
1 teaspoon ground cumin
$1/2$ teaspoon sesame oil
2 tablespoons finely chopped
fresh coriander leaves

Halve aubergine lengthways; place on oven tray. Bake in moderately hot oven about 35 minutes or until tender. Cool; remove and discard skin. Blend or process aubergine with remaining ingredients until smooth. Cover; refrigerate about 30 minutes.

STORE baba ghanoush can be made 3 days ahead and refrigerated, covered.

quick beetroot dip

SERVES 4
PREPARATION TIME 10 MINUTES
PER SERVING 0.6G FAT;
33 CALORIES (137KJ)

225g can sliced beetroot,
drained well
$1/4$ cup (60ml) low-fat plain
yogurt
1 teaspoon ground coriander
2 teaspoons ground cumin

Blend or process all ingredients until smooth.

STORE dip can be made 3 days ahead and refrigerated, covered.

bagel chips

SERVES 4
PREPARATION TIME 10 MINUTES
COOKING TIME 15 MINUTES
(PLUS COOLING TIME)
PER SERVING 5.3G FAT;
354 CALORIES (1481KJ)

Traditionally, bagels do not contain fat or animal products; these are the correct ones to use for this recipe.

4 bagels
3 teaspoons monounsaturated
or polyunsaturated oil
2 cloves garlic, crushed
$^1/_2$ teaspoon dried oregano leaves

1 Using a serrated or electric knife, cut bagels into very thin slices. Place slices in single layer on oven trays; lightly brush one side of each slice with combined oil, garlic and oregano.
2 Bake in moderately slow oven for about 15 minutes or until lightly browned; cool chips on trays.

STORE chips can be stored in an airtight container for a month.

caramelised onion and red lentil dip

MAKES 2¹/₂ CUPS
PREPARATION TIME 10 MINUTES
COOKING TIME 15 MINUTES
PER TABLESPOON 2G FAT;
37 CALORIES (153KJ)

³/₄ cup (150g) red lentils
2 cups (500ml) boiling water
2 cloves garlic, quartered
1 medium potato (200g),
chopped coarsely
¹/₄ cup (60ml) olive oil
2 medium brown onions (300g),
sliced thinly
¹/₂ teaspoon ground cumin
1 teaspoon ground coriander
¹/₄ teaspoon sweet paprika
2 tablespoons lemon juice

1 Combine lentils, the water, garlic and potato in medium saucepan; bring to a boil. Reduce heat; simmer, uncovered, about 15 minutes or until lentils soften, stirring occasionally.

2 Meanwhile, heat 2 tablespoons of the oil in medium frying pan; cook onion, stirring occasionally, about 8 minutes or until caramelised. Remove 2 tablespoons of the onion from pan; reserve. Add spices to pan; cook, stirring, until fragrant. Remove from heat; stir in juice.

3 Blend or process lentil mixture and onion with remaining oil until dip is smooth. Top with reserved onion; serve with toasted pide or pitta crisps, if desired.

chilli pizza rounds

MAKES 12
PREPARATION TIME 10 MINUTES
COOKING TIME 10 MINUTES
PER PIZZA 1.7G FAT;
66 CALORIES (277KJ)

2 tablespoons finely chopped fresh oregano
80g low-fat ricotta cheese
1 small fresh red chilli, deseeded, chopped finely
1 tablespoon no-added-salt tomato paste
6 slices wholemeal bread (270g)
2 tablespoons finely grated parmesan cheese
extra oregano leaves, to garnish

1   Combine oregano, ricotta, chilli and paste in medium bowl.
2   Cut two 5cm rounds from each slice of bread; place rounds
under hot grill until lightly browned on both sides.
3   Spread rounds with prepared cheese mixture; sprinkle with
parmesan. Place under hot grill for about 5 minutes or until cheese
has melted. Sprinkle with extra oregano leaves to serve.

STORE cook recipe just before serving.

snacks

vegetarian pizza

SERVES 2
PREPARATION TIME 20 MINUTES
(PLUS STANDING TIME)
COOKING TIME 25 MINUTES
PER SERVING 7.9G FAT;
580 CALORIES (2427KJ)

7g sachet (2 teaspoons) dried yeast
$1/2$ teaspoon sugar
$1/2$ cup (125ml) warm water
$1^{1}/2$ cups (225g) plain flour
1 teaspoon monounsaturated or polyunsaturated oil
$1/4$ cup (65g) no-added-salt tomato paste
$1/2$ cup (100g) canned red kidney beans, drained
1 small red onion (100g), sliced thinly
1 small courgette (90g), sliced thinly
1 small red pepper (150g), sliced thinly
4 button mushrooms, sliced thinly
$1/4$ cup (25g) grated light mozzarella cheese
1 tablespoon grated parmesan cheese
1 tablespoon fresh basil leaves

1 Place yeast with sugar in large bowl; stir in the water. Cover; stand in warm place for about 10 minutes or until mixture is frothy.
2 Sift flour into large bowl; stir in yeast mixture and oil. Mix to a firm dough.
3 Turn dough onto floured surface; knead for about 5 minutes or until dough is smooth and elastic.
4 Return dough to bowl; cover. Stand in warm place for about 45 minutes or until doubled in size. Turn dough onto lightly floured surface; knead until smooth.
5 Roll dough large enough to line 20cm pizza tray. Spread dough with paste; top with remaining ingredients, except basil. Bake in moderately hot oven for about 25 minutes or until crust is crisp. Serve pizza with basil leaves sprinkled on top.

STORE uncooked pizza can be prepared 3 hours ahead and refrigerated, covered.

mains

vegetable moussaka

SERVES 2
PREPARATION TIME 10 MINUTES
COOKING TIME 50 MINUTES
(PLUS COOLING TIME)
PER SERVING 6.1G FAT;
207 CALORIES (867KJ)

1 large aubergine (500g), sliced thickly
2 large tomatoes (500g), chopped finely
1 teaspoon sugar
2 teaspoons monounsaturated or polyunsaturated margarine
1 tablespoon plain flour
1 cup (250ml) skimmed milk
2 tablespoons finely grated parmesan cheese
2 tablespoons finely chopped fresh basil leaves

1 Place aubergine slices in single layer on oven tray; bake, uncovered, in a moderately hot oven for 15 minutes. Turn, bake for further 15 minutes or until browned lightly; cool for 10 minutes.
2 Combine tomato and sugar in small saucepan; cook, stirring occasionally, for about 30 minutes or until tomato is soft and liquid almost evaporated.
3 Meanwhile, melt margarine in small saucepan; add flour. Cook, stirring for 1 minute. Gradually add milk; stir over medium heat until sauce boils and thickens. Stir in half the cheese and half the basil. Stir remaining basil through tomato mixture.
4 Spread one-third of tomato mixture, aubergine and cheese sauce in two ovenproof dishes (2-cup capacity); repeat with two more layers. Sprinkle with remaining cheese.
5 Bake, uncovered, in moderate oven, about 15 minutes or until moussaka is lightly browned.

STORE moussaka can be prepared 3 hours ahead and refrigerated, covered.

roasted vegetable lasagne

SERVES 6
PREPARATION TIME 40 MINUTES
(PLUS STANDING TIME)
COOKING TIME 1 HOUR
PER SERVING 9G FAT
311 CALORIES (1300KJ)

3 medium red peppers (600g)
2 medium aubergines (600g), sliced thinly
2 tablespoons coarse cooking salt
2 medium courgettes (240g), sliced thinly
600g sweet potato, sliced thinly
cooking-oil spray
700g bottled tomato pasta sauce
4 fresh lasagne sheets
150g ricotta cheese, crumbled
1 tablespoon finely grated parmesan

WHITE SAUCE
40g low-fat dairy-free spread
1/4 cup (35g) plain flour
1 1/2 cups (375ml) skimmed milk
2 tablespoons coarsely grated parmesan

1 Preheat oven to very hot (240°C/220°C fan-assisted).
2 Quarter peppers; discard seeds and membranes. Roast, uncovered, in very hot oven, skin-side up, about 5 minutes or until skin blisters and blackens. Cover pepper pieces in plastic or paper for 5 minutes; peel away skin.
3 Reduce oven to moderately hot (200°C/180°C). Place aubergine in colander, sprinkle with salt; stand 20 minutes. Rinse aubergine under cold water; pat dry with absorbent paper.
4 Place aubergine, courgettes and sweet potato, in single layer, on oven trays; spray with oil. Roast, uncovered, about 15 minutes or until tender.
5 Meanwhile, make white sauce (see left).
6 Oil deep rectangular 2.5-litre (10-cup) ovenproof dish. Spread 1 cup pasta sauce over base of prepared dish; top with half of the aubergine and half of the pepper. Layer with lasagne sheet; top with half the remaining pasta sauce, ricotta, sweet potato and courgettes. Layer with another lasagne sheet; top with remaining pasta sauce, remaining aubergine and remaining pepper. Place remaining lasagne sheet over vegetables; top with white sauce, sprinkle with parmesan. Bake, uncovered, for about 45 minutes or until browned lightly. Stand 5 minutes before serving with a rocket salad.

WHITE SAUCE melt spread in small saucepan, add flour; cook, stirring, until mixture thickens and bubbles. Remove from heat, gradually stir in milk; cook, stirring, until sauce boils and thickens. Remove from heat; stir in cheese.

TIP use scissors to trim lasagne sheets to fit into your baking dish; you may only need three sheets in total.

pasta with pesto sauce

SERVES 2
PREPARATION TIME 10 MINUTES
COOKING TIME 10 MINUTES
PER SERVING 15.6G FAT;
600 CALORIES (2512KJ)

2 cups (160g) fresh basil leaves
1 clove garlic, crushed
$1/3$ cup (25g) grated parmesan cheese
1 tablespoon olive oil
1 tablespoon oil-free light French dressing
250g spaghetti pasta

1 Blend or process basil, garlic, cheese, oil and dressing until well combined.
2 Add pasta to large saucepan of boiling water. Boil, uncovered, until just tender; drain.
3 Toss pesto through pasta before serving.

STORE pesto can be made 3 days ahead and refrigerated, covered.

vegetable risotto

1 small aubergine (230g), chopped finely
salt
2 teaspoons olive oil
1 small brown onion (80g), chopped finely
1 clove garlic, crushed
3/4 cup (150g) brown rice
3/4 cup (80ml) chicken stock
2 cups (500ml) water
2 medium courgettes (240g)
2 medium tomatoes (380g), peeled, chopped finely
125g mushrooms, sliced thinly
1/4 cup (20g) coarsely grated parmesan cheese
1 tablespoon fresh oregano leaves

SERVES 2
PREPARATION TIME 10 MINUTES (PLUS STANDING TIME)
COOKING TIME 45 MINUTES
PER SERVING 11.2G FAT; 459 CALORIES (1923KJ)

1 Place aubergine in colander; sprinkle with salt. Stand for 30 minutes; rinse well under cold water. Pat dry with absorbent paper.
2 Heat oil in large saucepan; cook onion and garlic until soft. Add rice, stock and the water; bring to boil. Simmer, covered, for about 30 minutes or until rice is tender and almost all the liquid is absorbed.
3 Using a vegetable peeler, cut courgettes into ribbons.
4 Stir aubergine, courgettes, tomato and mushrooms into rice; cook for about 3 minutes or until vegetables are softened. Stir in half the cheese and oregano; serve risotto sprinkled with remaining cheese.

STORE risotto is best made just before serving.

artichoke risotto

SERVES 6
PREPARATION TIME 10 MINUTES
COOKING TIME 25 MINUTES
PER SERVING 4.5G FAT; 323 CALORIES (1353KJ)

While the short-grained arborio rice is traditionally used in a risotto, we chose to use long-grain rice here because it has both a lower GI rating and is more amenable to being cooked with the liquids added all at once.

2 teaspoons olive oil
1 medium brown onion (150g), chopped finely
3 cloves garlic, crushed
6 spring onions, sliced thinly
2 cups (400g) long-grain rice
$^3/_4$ cup (180ml) dry white wine
1$^1/_2$ cups (375ml) chicken stock
3 cups (750ml) water
400g can artichoke hearts, drained, sliced thinly
$^1/_2$ cup (40g) finely grated parmesan cheese

1 Heat oil in large saucepan; cook brown onion, garlic and half of the spring onion, stirring, until brown onion softens. Add rice, wine, stock and the water; bring to a boil. Reduce heat; simmer, covered, 15 minutes, stirring occasionally.
2 Stir in artichokes, cheese and remaining spring onion; cook, stirring, about 5 minutes or until artichokes are heated through.

TIP continue the Italian theme and serve the risotto with fresh slices of crusty ciabatta, if desired

SERVING SUGGESTION a salad of cherry tomatoes, sliced fennel and a few fresh basil leaves suits this risotto perfectly.

swiss chard, mushroom and pepper frittata

Swiss chard, also known as chard or silverbeet, is a leafy, dark green vegetable

SERVES 4
PREPARATION TIME 15 MINUTES
COOKING TIME 45 MINUTES
PER SERVING 6.7G FAT;
193 CALORIES (809KJ)

500g Swiss chard, trimmed, chopped coarsely
1 tablespoon low-fat dairy-free spread
1 medium brown onion (150g), chopped finely
2 cloves garlic, crushed
1 medium red pepper (200g), chopped finely
2 sticks celery (150g), trimmed and chopped finely
100g button mushrooms, sliced thinly
2 large carrots (360g), grated coarsely
$1/4$ cup (40g) polenta
$1/4$ cup coarsely chopped fresh basil
3 eggs, beaten lightly
3 egg whites, beaten lightly
$1/3$ cup (80ml) skimmed milk

1 Preheat oven to moderate.
2 Line a 20cm x 30cm shallow rectangular baking pan with baking parchment.
3 Boil, steam or microwave Swiss chard; drain on absorbent paper.
4 Melt spread in large deep frying pan; cook onion and garlic, stirring, until onion softens. Add pepper, celery and mushrooms; cook, stirring, until vegetables just soften.
5 Stir Swiss chard, carrot, polenta and basil into vegetable mixture. Remove from heat; cool 5 minutes. Add eggs, whites and milk; stir to combine. Spread frittata mixture into prepared pan; bake, uncovered, in moderate oven about 35 minutes or until lightly browned and firm to the touch.

TIP this frittata is just as good eaten at room temperature as it is hot from the oven.

SERVING SUGGESTION
serve frittata with a salad of mixed grape, cherry and baby plum tomatoes.

leek, spinach and mushroom frittata

This Italian interpretation of a low-fat vegetable omelette simplifies the cooking process by oven-baking, rather than completing it on the stove-top.

SERVES 6
PREPARATION TIME 15 MINUTES
COOKING TIME 40 MINUTES
PER SERVING 3.0G FAT;
91 CALORIES (380KJ)

1 teaspoon low-fat dairy-free spread
3 cloves garlic, crushed
1 small leek (200g), sliced thinly
400g button mushrooms, sliced thickly
200g baby spinach leaves
2 eggs
6 egg whites
$^1/_2$ cup (125ml) skimmed milk
$^1/_2$ cup (40g) coarsely grated low-fat cheddar cheese

1 Preheat oven to moderately low.
2 Oil a deep 23cm-round cake tin. Line base with baking parchment.
3 Melt dairy-free spread in medium frying pan; cook garlic and leek, stirring, until leek softens. Add mushrooms; cook, stirring, until mushrooms are just tender. Add spinach; cook, stirring, until spinach just wilts. Drain off and discard any liquid.
4 Using whisk, combine eggs, egg whites, milk and cheese in large bowl; stir in vegetable mixture.
5 Pour egg mixture into prepared tin. Bake in moderately slow oven about 30 minutes or until just set. Place frittata under hot grill until browned.

SERVING SUGGESTION
serve with a salad of sliced tomatoes and shredded basil.

TIP use brown mushrooms as an alternative tasty mushroom.

mains

egg-white omelette

SERVES 4
PREPARATION TIME 10 MINUTES
COOKING TIME 15 MINUTES
PER SERVING 6.3G FAT;
303 CALORIES (1268KJ)

150g lean ham
200g button mushrooms, sliced thinly
12 egg whites
$1/4$ cup finely chopped fresh chives
2 medium tomatoes (380g), chopped coarsely
$1/2$ cup (45g) coarsely grated low-fat cheddar cheese
8 slices wholemeal bread

1 Trim and discard any fat from ham; cut into thin strips. Cook ham in heated large non-stick frying pan, stirring, until lightly browned. Remove from pan. Cook mushrooms in same pan, stirring, until lightly browned.

2 Using electric mixer, beat 3 of the egg whites in small bowl until soft peaks form; fold in a quarter of the chives. Preheat grill. Pour egg-white mixture into heated lightly oiled non-stick 20cm frying pan; cook, uncovered, over low heat until just browned underneath. Place pan under preheated grill; cook until top just sets. Place a quarter of the tomato on one half of the omelette; return to grill, cook until tomato is hot and top is lightly browned. Gently place a quarter of each of the cheese, ham and mushroom on tomato half of omelette; fold over to enclose filling. Carefully transfer omelette to serving plate; cover to keep warm.

3 Repeat step 2 with remaining egg whites, chives and fillings.

4 Toast bread until lightly browned both sides. Serve omelettes with toast.

salmon and herb soufflés

SERVES 2
PREPARATION TIME 10 MINUTES
COOKING TIME 25 MINUTES
PER SERVING 14.3G FAT;
257 CALORIES (1075KJ)

210g canned salmon, drained
1 tablespoon finely chopped fresh chives
1 tablespoon finely chopped fresh parsley
pinch cayenne pepper
1 tablespoon monounsaturated or polyunsaturated margarine
1 tablespoon plain flour
$^1/_2$ cup (125ml) skimmed milk
2 egg whites

1 Grease two soufflé dishes (1 cup capacity). Combine salmon, herbs and pepper in large bowl; mix well.
2 Heat margarine in medium saucepan; stir in flour. Cook until bubbling; remove from heat. Gradually stir in milk; stir over heat until sauce boils and thickens. Stir sauce into salmon mixture.
3 Beat egg whites until soft peaks form; fold into salmon mixture. Spoon mixture into prepared dishes.
4 Bake in moderate oven for about 20 minutes or until risen and well browned.

STORE cook recipe just before serving.

salmon rice paper rolls

Wasabi is available in both paste and powdered forms. We used the paste but, if you add a few drops of cold water to the powder, as instructed on the label, you can use this mixture as a substitute.

SERVES 4
PREPARATION TIME 30 MINUTES
(PLUS STANDING TIME)
PER ROLL 4G FAT;
108 CALORIES (452KJ)

50g rice vermicelli
250g thin fresh asparagus spears
12 x 22cm-round rice paper sheets
$1/3$ cup (80ml) light soured cream
2 teaspoons finely chopped fresh dill
$1/4$ teaspoon wasabi
2 teaspoons finely grated lemon rind
400g thinly sliced smoked salmon
1 small red onion (100g), sliced finely
60g mangetout sprouts

1 Place vermicelli in medium heatproof bowl; cover with boiling water. Stand until just tender; drain.
2 Boil, steam or microwave asparagus until just tender; drain. Trim ends – asparagus should be 15cm long.
3 Place 1 sheet of rice paper in medium bowl of warm water until just softened. Lift from water carefully; place on board.
4 Combine soured cream, dill, wasabi and lemon rind in small bowl.
5 Place 1 slice of salmon on one edge of rice paper, towards the centre. Spread with soured cream mixture, top with 2 asparagus spears, onion, sprouts and vermicelli. Fold rice paper over filling. Roll up to enclose filling; one end will remain open.
6 Repeat with remaining rice paper rounds and filling.

STORE make recipe just before serving.

salmon patties with baby spinach

Baby spinach leaves, along with baby rocket, are the greens of choice for many people today. And why not? They can be used in everything from salads to stir-fries to soups, with no preparation or pre-cooking required; they're full of nutrients; and their respective singular flavours add something special to the dishes in which they are used.

SERVES 8
PREPARATION TIME 30 MINUTES
COOKING TIME 45 MINUTES
PER SERVING 7.2G FAT;
287 CALORIES (1203KJ)

5 medium potatoes (1kg), chopped coarsely
415g canned red salmon, drained and flaked
6 spring onions, chopped finely
2 sticks celery (150g), trimmed and grated coarsely
1 teaspoon finely grated lemon rind
$^{1}/_{3}$ cup (80ml) lemon juice
2 egg whites
2 tablespoons water
2 cups (200g) packaged breadcrumbs
1 teaspoon vegetable oil
230g can sliced water chestnuts, drained
600g baby spinach leaves
1 tablespoon light soy sauce
$^{1}/_{4}$ cup (60ml) mirin
2 teaspoons sugar

1 Preheat oven to very hot.
2 Boil, steam or microwave potato until tender; drain. Mash potato in large bowl until smooth; cool slightly. Stir in salmon, onion, celery, rind and half of the juice.
3 Using floured hands, shape fish mixture into 16 patties. Dip patties, one at a time, in combined egg white and water, then in breadcrumbs. Place patties on lightly oiled oven tray. Cover and refrigerate for 30 minutes.
4 Cook patties, uncovered, in very hot oven about 30 minutes or until golden brown and heated through.
5 Meanwhile, heat oil in wok or large non-stick frying pan; stir-fry water chestnuts for 1 minute. Add spinach, remaining juice, sauce, mirin and sugar; stir-fry until spinach just wilts. Top spinach with salmon patties to serve.

SERVING SUGGESTION
accompany patties and
spinach with tomato or
sweet onion relish and
sliced light rye bread.

oven-steamed sea trout

SERVES 4
PREPARATION TIME 10 MINUTES
COOKING TIME 15 MINUTES
PER SERVING 7.9G FAT;
418 CALORIES (1751KJ)

4 x 200g sea trout fillets
2 tablespoons lemon juice
1 tablespoon drained capers, chopped
coarsely
2 teaspoons coarsely chopped fresh dill
1.2kg large new potatoes, sliced thickly

1 Preheat oven to moderately hot.
2 Place each fillet on a square of foil large
enough to completely enclose fish; top
each fillet with equal amounts of juice,
capers and dill. Gather corners of foil
squares together above fish, twist to
close securely.
3 Place parcels on oven tray; cook in
moderately hot oven about 15 minutes
or until fish is cooked as desired. Unwrap
and remove fish from foil before serving.
4 Meanwhile, boil, steam or microwave
potato until tender. Serve fish with potato.

SERVING SUGGESTION
accompany trout with
mixed salad leaves.

TIPS use tweezers to remove any bones
from fish. Rinse and drain capers before
using to rid them of excess salt or brine

cantonese steamed ginger snapper

SERVES 4
PREPARATION TIME 10 MINUTES
COOKING TIME 30 MINUTES
PER SERVING 3.2G FAT;
137 CALORIES (573KJ)

40g piece ginger
4 small whole snapper (1.2kg)
1/4 cup (60ml) vegetable stock
4 spring onions, sliced thinly
1/2 cup tightly packed fresh
coriander leaves
1/3 cup (80ml) salt-reduced
light soy sauce
1 teaspoon sesame oil

If snapper is unavailable, use your favourite whole firm-fleshed fish for this recipe.

1 Peel ginger; cut into thin strips lengthways, then cut into match-stick-size pieces.
2 Score fish three times both sides; place each fish on a separate large sheet of foil. Sprinkle with ginger and drizzle with half the stock; fold foil loosely to enclose fish.
3 Place fish in large bamboo steamer; steam fish, covered, over wok or large frying pan of simmering water for about 30 minutes or until cooked through.
4 Transfer fish to serving dish; sprinkle with onion and coriander, then drizzle with combined remaining stock, sauce and oil. Serve with steamed broccoli and baby corn, if desired.

STORE cook recipe just before serving.

mains

63

fish kebabs with chilli sauce

SERVES 2
PREPARATION TIME 15 MINUTES
(PLUS MARINATING TIME)
COOKING TIME 15 MINUTES
PER SERVING 10.8G FAT;
469 CALORIES (1964KJ)

You will need to cook about $^1/_3$ cup (65g) long-grain rice for this recipe.

300g tuna steaks, cut into 3cm pieces
1 tablespoon salt-reduced soy sauce
1 clove garlic, crushed
$^1/_4$ teaspoon grated fresh ginger
1 medium red pepper (200g), chopped coarsely
1 medium green pepper (200g), chopped coarsely
2 teaspoons monounsaturated or polyunsaturated oil
1 cup cooked long-grain rice

CHILLI SAUCE
1 small fresh red chilli, chopped finely
2 cloves garlic, crushed
1 tablespoon finely chopped fresh coriander leaves
1 tablespoon fish sauce
1 tablespoon lime juice
$1^1/_2$ tablespoons brown sugar
1 tablespoon mirin
$^1/_3$ cup (80ml) water

1 Combine fish with sauce, garlic and ginger in large bowl; refrigerate for 1 hour.
2 Thread fish and pepper alternately onto 4 skewers. Brush with oil; cook under hot grill until fish is tender. Serve kebabs on rice topped with sauce.

CHILLI SAUCE grind chilli, garlic and coriander to a smooth paste. Add fish sauce, juice, sugar, mirin and the water. Transfer mixture to small saucepan; stir until sugar is dissolved and sauce heated through.

STORE fish can be marinated a day ahead and refrigerated, covered.

garlic prawns and bok choy with herbed rice

Traditional garlic prawns are given a Southeast-Asian tweak in this stir-fry. Bok choy has become as common a vegetable staple as green beans or broccoli in most kitchens, and not without good reason. It's versatile, easy to cook, keeps well … and is delicious.

SERVES 6
PREPARATION TIME 20 MINUTES
COOKING TIME 15 MINUTES
PER SERVING 4.5G FAT;
383 CALORIES (1602KJ)

36 medium uncooked prawns (1kg)
6 cloves garlic, crushed
2 teaspoons finely chopped fresh coriander
3 red thai chillies, deseeded, chopped finely
$1/3$ cup (80ml) lime juice
1 teaspoon sugar
1 tablespoon peanut oil
1kg baby bok choy, quartered lengthways
6 spring onions, sliced thinly
1 tablespoon sweet chilli sauce

HERBED RICE
2 cups (400g) jasmine rice
2 tablespoons coarsely chopped fresh coriander
1 tablespoon coarsely chopped fresh mint
1 tablespoon coarsely chopped fresh flat-leaf parsley
1 teaspoon finely grated lime rind

1 Shell and devein prawns, leaving tails intact.
2 Combine prawns in large bowl with garlic, coriander, chilli, juice and sugar.
3 Heat half of the oil in wok or large non-stick frying pan; stir-fry prawns, in batches, until just changed in colour.
4 Heat remaining oil with pan liquids in wok; stir-fry bok choy, onion and sauce, in batches, until just tender. Combine bok choy mixture and prawns in wok; stir-fry until hot. Serve prawns on herbed rice.

HERBED RICE cook rice, uncovered, in large saucepan of boiling water until tender; drain. Return rice to pan; combine with remaining ingredients.

chorizo stuffed roast chicken

SERVES 4
PREPARATION TIME 25 MINUTES
COOKING TIME 1 HOUR 35 MINUTES
PER SERVING 68.4G FAT;
967 CALORIES (4042KJ)

20g butter
1 medium brown onion (150g), chopped finely
1 chorizo sausage (170g), diced into 1cm pieces
1^1/$_2$ cups (110g) stale breadcrumbs
^{1}/$_2$ cup (100g) ricotta cheese
1 egg
^{1}/$_4$ cup finely chopped fresh flat-leaf parsley
^{1}/$_4$ cup (35g) toasted slivered almonds
1.6kg chicken
2 medium lemons (280g), cut into wedges

SPINACH AND RED ONION SALAD
150g baby spinach leaves
1 small red onion (100g), sliced thinly
1 tablespoon red wine vinegar
2 tablespoons olive oil

1 Melt half of the butter in medium frying pan; cook onion and chorizo, stirring, until onion softens. Cool 10 minutes; combine chorizo mixture in medium bowl with breadcrumbs, ricotta, egg, parsley and nuts.
2 Preheat oven to moderately hot (200°C/180°C fan-assisted).
3 Wash chicken under cold water; pat dry inside and out with absorbent paper. Tuck wing tips under chicken. Trim skin around neck; secure neck flap to underside of chicken with skewers.
4 Fill cavity with chorizo mixture, fold over skin to enclose stuffing; secure with toothpicks. Tie legs together with string. Place chicken and lemon in medium baking dish. Rub chicken all over with remaining butter; roast, uncovered, about 1^1/$_2$ hours or until chicken is cooked through, basting occasionally with juices.
5 Meanwhile, place ingredients for spinach and red onion salad in large bowl; toss gently to combine.
6 Serve chicken with stuffing, lemon and salad.

spanish chicken casserole

SERVES 4
PREPARATION TIME 10 MINUTES
COOKING TIME 1 HOUR 25 MINUTES
PER SERVING 61.4G FAT;
969 CALORIES (4050KJ)

1 tablespoon olive oil
4 chicken drumsticks (600g)
4 chicken thigh cutlets (800g)
1 large brown onion (200g), chopped finely
4 medium potatoes (800g), quartered
$^1/_2$ cup (80g) toasted pine nuts
$^1/_2$ cup (80g) toasted blanched almonds
3 cups (750ml) chicken stock
1 cup (250ml) dry white wine
$^1/_3$ cup (80ml) lemon juice
4 cloves garlic, crushed
2 tablespoons fresh thyme leaves
$^1/_2$ cup coarsely chopped fresh flat-leaf parsley
500g fine green beans, trimmed

1 Preheat oven to moderate (180°C/160°C fan-assisted).
2 Heat oil in large flameproof casserole dish; cook chicken, in batches, until browned.
3 Cook onion in same dish, stirring, until soft. Return chicken to dish with potato, nuts, stock, wine, juice, garlic, thyme and half of the parsley; bring to a boil. Cover; cook in oven about 1 hour or until chicken is cooked through.
4 Meanwhile, boil, steam or microwave beans until tender; drain.
5 Serve chicken with beans; sprinkle with remaining parsley.

TIP when using wine in cooking, as a general rule of thumb you should never cook with a wine you wouldn't drink; the wine you use doesn't have to be expensive, but it does have to be drinkable. If you don't want to use white wine, you could substitute water, ginger ale or white grape juice.

chicken and lentil cacciatore

cooking-oil spray
8 skinless chicken thigh fillets
(880g), halved
1 medium brown onion (150g),
chopped finely
300g button mushrooms, halved
1 clove garlic, crushed
2 x 440g cans no-added-salt tomatoes
1 tablespoon no-added-salt tomato paste
1 cup (250ml) chicken stock
$^1/_3$ cup (65g) red lentils
$^1/_2$ cup (60g) pitted black olives
1 tablespoon drained capers
2 teaspoons finely chopped fresh oregano
2 tablespoons finely chopped fresh parsley

SERVES 4
PREPARATION TIME 15 MINUTES
COOKING TIME 40 MINUTES
PER SERVING 17.3G FAT; 444 CALORIES (1858KJ)

1 Lightly spray large non-stick saucepan with cooking-oil spray.
Cook chicken until browned all over, turning occasionally. Remove
from pan.
2 Add onion, mushrooms and garlic to pan; cook, stirring, until onion
is soft. Add undrained crushed tomatoes, paste, stock and lentils.
3 Return chicken to pan; simmer, covered, for about 30 minutes or
until chicken is tender. Stir in olives, capers, oregano and parsley.

STORE recipe can be made a day ahead and refrigerated, covered,
or frozen.

ginger chicken kebabs

300g chicken breast fillets,
chopped coarsely
1 tablespoon green ginger wine
1 tablespoon salt-reduced soy sauce
1 tablespoon lemon juice
1 teaspoon monounsaturated or
polyunsaturated oil
2 teaspoons Worcestershire sauce
2 teaspoons brown sugar
1 teaspoon Dijon mustard
1 teaspoon grated fresh ginger

SERVES 2
PREPARATION TIME 15 MINUTES
(PLUS MARINATING TIME)
COOKING TIME 15 MINUTES
PER SERVING 10.6G FAT; 261 CALORIES (1091KJ)

1 Combine chicken and all the remaining ingredients in large bowl;
refrigerate for several hours or overnight.
2 Thread chicken onto skewers; reserve marinade. Grill kebabs,
brushing with marinade, until chicken is tender. Serve sprinkled with
sliced spring onions, if desired.

STORE chicken is best marinated a day ahead and refrigerated,
covered.

mains

chicken, lemon and artichoke skewers

SERVES 4
PREPARATION TIME 20 MINUTES
COOKING TIME 10 MINUTES
PER SERVING 22.6G FAT;
366 CALORIES (1534KJ)

3 medium lemons (420g)
2 cloves garlic, crushed
$^1/_4$ cup (60ml) olive oil
600g chicken breast fillets, chopped coarsely
800g canned artichoke hearts, drained and halved
24 button mushrooms

1 Squeeze juice from one lemon (you will need two tablespoons of juice). Combine juice, garlic and oil in small screw-top jar; shake well.
2 Cut remaining lemons into 24 wedges. Thread chicken, artichoke, mushrooms and lemon onto 12 skewers. (They can be made a day ahead to this stage and refrigerated, covered.)
3 Cook skewers on heated oiled grill plate (or grill or barbecue) until browned all over and cooked through. Brush with oil mixture during cooking.

grilled tandoori chicken

SERVES 2
PREPARATION TIME 10 MINUTES
(PLUS MARINATING TIME)
COOKING TIME 15 MINUTES
PER SERVING 12.5G FAT;
348 CALORIES (1457KJ)

$^1/_2$ cup (125ml) low-fat plain yogurt
1 tablespoon lemon juice
$^1/_2$ teaspoon finely grated fresh ginger
1 clove garlic, crushed
$^1/_2$ teaspoon caster sugar
$^1/_2$ teaspoon paprika
$^1/_4$ teaspoon ground cumin
$^1/_4$ teaspoon ground coriander
$^1/_4$ teaspoon ground turmeric
pinch chilli powder
2 x 200g single chicken breast fillets

TOMATO, RED ONION AND CORIANDER SALSA
1 small tomato (130g), chopped finely
$^1/_4$ small red onion (50g), chopped finely
1 teaspoon sugar
1 tablespoon finely chopped fresh coriander leaves

1 Combine yogurt, juice, ginger, garlic, sugar, paprika and spices in large bowl. Add chicken; turn chicken to coat in marinade. Refrigerate for several hours or overnight.
2 Grill chicken, brushing with marinade, until browned on both sides and tender. Serve chicken sliced thickly, with tomato, red onion and coriander salsa, and steamed rice, if desired.

TOMATO, RED ONION AND CORIANDER SALSA combine all ingredients in small bowl.

STORE chicken is best marinated a day ahead and refrigerated, covered.

herb-crusted lamb racks with new potatoes and leek

SERVES 4
PREPARATION TIME 25 MINUTES
COOKING TIME 55 MINUTES
(PLUS STANDING TIME)
PER SERVING 13.7G FAT;
437 CALORIES (1829KJ)

4 x 3-cutlet racks of lamb (900g)
$^1/_4$ cup (20g) fresh white breadcrumbs
1 tablespoon finely chopped fresh rosemary
1 tablespoon finely chopped fresh flat-leaf parsley
2 teaspoons finely chopped fresh thyme
3 cloves garlic, crushed
3 teaspoons bottled coriander pesto
1kg new potatoes, halved lengthways
vegetable-oil spray
1 teaspoon sea salt
2 medium leeks (700g), trimmed
2 teaspoons low-fat dairy-free spread
$^1/_4$ cup (60ml) chicken stock
$^1/_4$ cup (60ml) dry white wine

1 Preheat oven to moderately hot.
2 Remove any excess fat from lamb. Combine breadcrumbs, herbs, garlic and pesto in small bowl. Using hands, press breadcrumb mixture onto lamb racks, cover; refrigerate until required.
3 Place potatoes in large shallow baking dish; spray with oil, sprinkle with salt. Roast, uncovered, in moderately hot oven 20 minutes.
4 Place lamb on top of the potatoes; roast, uncovered, in moderately hot oven 10 minutes. Reduce heat to slow; cook about 20 minutes or until potatoes are tender and lamb is cooked as desired.
5 Meanwhile, cut leeks into 10cm lengths; slice thinly lengthways. Melt spread in large frying pan; cook leek, stirring, until it softens. Stir in stock and wine; bring to a boil. Reduce heat; simmer, uncovered, until liquid reduces by half.
6 Stand lamb for 5 minutes before cutting racks into cutlets; serve cutlets with potatoes and leek.

SERVING SUGGESTION
mesclun with a lemon and rosemary-scented vinaigrette marries with this main course beautifully.

TIP herbed breadcrumb mixture can be patted onto racks the day before serving. Cover and refrigerate overnight.

mains

pepper-grilled lamb fillets with roasted root vegetables

All manner of baby vegetables are available at better greengrocers and some supermarkets. You could also serve baby cauliflower, baby turnips and baby pumpkin with the lamb in this recipe.

SERVES 8
PREPARATION TIME 30 MINUTES
COOKING TIME 1 HOUR
PER SERVING 4.8G FAT;
293 CALORIES (1228KJ)

1kg baby beetroots, trimmed
6 small parsnips (360g), quartered
500g baby new potatoes, halved
400g baby carrots, trimmed
8 baby onions (200g), halved
4 cloves garlic, peeled
$^1/_4$ cup (60ml) orange juice
$^1/_4$ cup (90g) honey
1 tablespoon seeded mustard
12 lamb fillets (960g)
$1^1/_2$ tablespoons cracked black pepper

1 Preheat oven to moderately hot.
2 Boil, steam or microwave unpeeled beetroot until tender; drain. When cool enough to handle, peel beetroot.
3 Combine beetroot in large lightly oiled baking dish with parsnips, potatoes, carrots, onions and garlic. Pour combined juice, honey and mustard over vegetables; roast, uncovered, in moderately hot oven, stirring occasionally, about 45 minutes or until vegetables are browned and tender.
4 Meanwhile, coat lamb all over with pepper. Cook lamb on heated oiled grill plate (or grill or barbecue) until browned all over and cooked as desired. Cover; stand 10 minutes. Slice thickly.
5 Serve vegetables topped with lamb.

SERVING SUGGESTION
accompany this recipe with bowl of lemon-scented steamed couscous.

lamb hot pot with couscous

SERVES 2
PREPARATION TIME 15 MINUTES
(PLUS STANDING TIME)
COOKING TIME 45 MINUTES
PER SERVING 20.3G FAT;
871 CALORIES (3648KJ)

600g lamb leg chops
1 tablespoon plain flour
2 teaspoons olive oil
1 medium brown onion (150g), cut into thin wedges
1 teaspoon ground cinnamon
1 teaspoon ground turmeric
1 cup (250ml) water
$1/2$ cup (125ml) beef stock
100g prunes, pitted
2 tablespoons finely chopped fresh coriander leaves

COUSCOUS
1 cup (250ml) boiling water
1 cup (200g) couscous

1 Trim all visible fat from lamb. Cut lamb into cubes; toss in flour.
2 Heat oil in large saucepan; cook onion until soft. Add lamb; cook until lamb is browned all over. Stir in cinnamon and turmeric; cook for 1 minute.
3 Stir in the water, stock and prunes; bring to boil. Simmer, covered, for about 30 minutes or until lamb is tender. Serve lamb with couscous, sprinkled with coriander.

COUSCOUS pour the water over couscous in medium bowl; stand for 5 minutes or until liquid is absorbed. Stir with a fork.

STORE hot pot can be made a day ahead and refrigerated, covered. Couscous is best made close to serving time.

lamb patties with beetroot and tzatziki

Use the outer leaves of the lettuce for this recipe. The patties and yogurt mixture can be prepared several hours ahead.

SERVES 4
PREPARATION TIME 20 MINUTES
COOKING TIME 10 MINUTES
PER SERVING 14.9G FAT;
296 CALORIES (1240KJ)

500g lamb mince
1 small brown onion (80g), chopped finely
1 medium carrot (120g), grated coarsely
1 egg, beaten lightly
2 tablespoons finely chopped fresh flat-leaf parsley
2 cloves garlic, crushed
1 teaspoon grated lemon rind
$1/2$ teaspoon dried oregano
$1/2$ cup (140g) plain yogurt
1 cucumber (130g), deseeded and chopped finely
1 tablespoon chopped fresh mint
1 large pitta bread
outer leaves of cos lettuce, shredded
400g canned whole baby beetroot, drained and quartered

1 Combine lamb, onion, carrot, egg, parsley, 1 clove of garlic, rind and oregano in large bowl; mix well. Shape mixture into 8 patties.
2 Cook patties on heated oiled grill plate or barbecue, in batches, until browned on both sides and cooked as desired.
3 Meanwhile, combine yogurt, remaining garlic, cucumber and mint in small bowl; mix well. Cut bread into four even pieces, split each piece in half crossways; toast, cut-side up, until browned lightly.
4 Just before serving, sandwich bread with lettuce leaves, patties, yogurt mixture and beetroot.

steak diane

SERVES 4
PREPARATION TIME 10 MINUTES
COOKING TIME 15 MINUTES
PER SERVING 51.1G FAT;
658 CALORIES (2755KJ)

1 tablespoon olive oil
8 thin slices beef fillet (800g)
20g butter
3 cloves garlic, crushed
3 spring onions, sliced thinly
1 tablespoon brandy
2 tablespoons Worcestershire sauce
300ml cream

SERVING SUGGESTION
serve steak diane with
french fries.

1 Heat oil in large frying pan; cook beef, in batches, until browned both sides and cooked as desired. Cover to keep warm.
2 Melt butter in same pan; cook garlic and onion, stirring, until onion softens. Add brandy and sauce; bring to a boil. Stir in cream, reduce heat; simmer, uncovered, about 3 minutes or until sauce thickens slightly.
3 Divide beef equally among serving plates; top with sauce.

mains

beef in red wine

SERVES 2
PREPARATION TIME 15 MINUTES
COOKING TIME 1¼ HOURS
PER SERVING 8G FAT;
408 CALORIES (1708KJ)

350g braising steak
2 medium brown onions (300g), chopped finely
1 clove garlic, crushed
100g mushrooms, sliced thickly
415ml canned tomato puree
2 teaspoons Worcestershire sauce
$1/2$ cup (125ml) dry red wine
1 stick celery (75g), trimmed and chopped coarsely
2 medium carrots (240g), chopped coarsely
2 tablespoons fresh parsley leaves

1 Trim all visible fat from steak; cut into cubes. Cook steak in heated large non-stick saucepan until browned all over. Add onion, garlic and mushrooms; cook, stirring, for about 2 minutes or until onion is soft. Stir in puree, sauce and wine; bring to boil. Simmer, covered, about 45 minutes.
2 Add celery and carrots; cook, covered, for a further 15 minutes or until vegetables are tender. Serve sprinkled with parsley. Serve with couscous, if desired.

STORE recipe can be made a day ahead and refrigerated, covered.

beef, red wine and chilli casserole with polenta

SERVES 4
PREPARATION TIME 15 MINUTES
COOKING TIME 1 HOUR 45 MINUTES
PER SERVING 14.3G FAT;
492 CALORIES (2058KJ)

2 teaspoons low-fat dairy-free spread
1.5kg lean beef chuck steak, cut into 3cm pieces
2 cloves garlic, crushed
3 red thai chillies, deseeded and sliced thinly
2 teaspoons Dijon mustard
1 large brown onion (200g), sliced thickly
2 medium tomatoes (380g), chopped coarsely
410g canned tomato purée
3/4 cup (180ml) dry red wine
1/2 cup (125ml) beef stock
1.125 litres (4 1/2 cups) water
1 cup (170g) polenta
1/4 cup (20g) finely grated parmesan cheese
2 tablespoons coarsely chopped fresh flat-leaf parsley

1 Melt spread in large saucepan; cook beef, in batches, until browned all over. Cook garlic, chilli, mustard and onion in same pan, stirring, until onion softens. Return beef to pan with tomato; cook, stirring, 2 minutes.
2 Add purée, wine, stock and 1/2 cup of the water to pan; bring to a boil. Reduce heat; simmer, covered, about 1 hour 30 minutes or until beef is tender, stirring occasionally.
3 Meanwhile, bring the remaining litre of water to a boil in medium saucepan. Add polenta; cook, stirring, over medium heat about 10 minutes or until thickened. Stir cheese into polenta.
4 Stir parsley into beef casserole just before serving with polenta.

SERVING SUGGESTION
serve with baby rocket leaves and sprinkled with flaked parmesan and a squeeze of lemon juice, if desired.

TIP as long as the wine you use is good enough to drink with the meal, any dry red will suffice; however, in keeping with the Italian feel of this recipe, we used a Chianti.

meatballs in rosemary paprika sauce

SERVES 2
PREPARATION TIME 15 MINUTES
COOKING TIME 45 MINUTES
PER SERVING 14.5G FAT;
880 CALORIES (3685KJ)

250g lean minced beef
$1/2$ cup (35g) stale breadcrumbs
1 tablespoon finely chopped fresh parsley
1 tablespoon finely chopped fresh chives
1 egg white
1 teaspoon Worcestershire sauce
1 teaspoon monounsaturated or polyunsaturated oil
250g tagliatelle pasta

ROSEMARY PAPRIKA SAUCE
410g can no-added-salt tomatoes
1 cup (250ml) water
2 tablespoons dry red wine
1 medium brown onion (150g), chopped finely
$1/2$ teaspoon Worcestershire sauce
1 teaspoon paprika
3 sprigs rosemary

1 Combine mince, breadcrumbs, parsley, chives, egg white and sauce in large bowl. Shape mixture into small meatballs.
2 Heat oil in medium non-stick saucepan; cook meatballs until well browned all over and cooked through. Drain on absorbent paper.
3 Cook pasta in large saucepan of boiling water until tender; drain.
4 Add meatballs to sauce; mix well. Stir until heated through. Serve with pasta and a crisp green leaf salad, if desired.

ROSEMARY PAPRIKA SAUCE combine undrained crushed tomatoes with remaining ingredients in medium saucepan; bring to boil. Simmer, uncovered, for about 20 minutes or until thickened slightly. Remove and discard rosemary sprigs.

STORE recipe can be made a day ahead and refrigerated, covered, or frozen. Cook pasta close to serving.

beef and onion kebabs

SERVES 2
PREPARATION TIME 20 MINUTES
(PLUS MARINATING TIME)
COOKING TIME 10 MINUTES
PER SERVING 8.3G FAT;
428 CALORIES (1794KJ)

350g lean rump steak
9 baby onions (225g), halved

MARINADE
$^1/_4$ cup (60ml) honey
$^1/_4$ cup (60ml) lemon juice
2 teaspoons grated fresh ginger
2 teaspoons Worcestershire sauce
$^1/_4$ cup (60ml) no-added-salt tomato sauce
1 tablespoon finely chopped fresh oregano leaves

1 Remove all visible fat from steak; chop steak into bite-size pieces.
Thread steak and onion onto six skewers.
2 Place kebabs in shallow dish; add marinade. Refrigerate overnight.
3 Cook kebabs on heated grill pan or barbecue, brushing with
marinade, until meat is tender. Serve with green leaf salad, if desired.

MARINADE combine all ingredients in bowl; mix well.

STORE cook marinated kebabs just before serving.

beef and bean tacos

SERVES 4
PREPARATION TIME 15 MINUTES COOKING TIME 20 MINUTES
PER SERVING 4.6G FAT; 156 CALORIES (654KJ)

1 clove garlic, crushed
80g lean minced beef
$1/2$ teaspoon chilli powder
$1/4$ teaspoon ground cumin
300g can kidney beans, rinsed and drained
2 tablespoons tomato paste
$1/2$ cup (125ml) water
1 medium tomato (190g), chopped coarsely
4 taco shells
$1/4$ small iceberg lettuce, shredded finely

SALSA CRUDA
$1/2$ cucumber (65g), deseeded and chopped finely
$1/2$ small red onion (40g), chopped finely
1 small tomato (130g), deseeded and chopped finely
1 teaspoon mild chilli sauce

1 Preheat oven to moderate.
2 Heat large lightly oiled non-stick frying pan; cook garlic and beef, stirring, until beef is browned all over. Add chilli, cumin, beans, paste, the water and tomato; cook, covered, over low heat about 15 minutes or until mixture thickens slightly.
3 Meanwhile, toast taco shells, upside-down and uncovered, on oven tray in moderate oven for 5 minutes.
4 Just before serving, fill taco shells with beef mixture, lettuce and salsa cruda.

SALSA CRUDA combine ingredients in small bowl.

red beef curry

SERVES 4
PREPARATION TIME **10 MINUTES**
COOKING TIME **20 MINUTES**
PER SERVING **41.9G FAT;**
571 CALORIES (2390KJ)

2 tablespoons peanut oil
500g beef rump, cut into 2cm pieces
1 large brown onion (200g),
sliced thinly
$^1/_4$ cup (75g) red curry paste
1 large red pepper (350g), sliced thinly
150g green beans, chopped
1$^2/_3$ cups (400ml) coconut milk
425g can crushed tomatoes
$^1/_4$ cup coarsely chopped fresh
coriander

1 Heat half of the oil in wok or large
frying pan; stir-fry beef, in batches, until
browned all over.
2 Heat remaining oil in same wok;
stir-fry onion until soft. Add paste;
stir-fry until fragrant. Add pepper and
green beans; stir-fry until vegetables
just soften.
3 Return beef to wok with remaining
ingredients; stir-fry until sauce thickens
slightly.

SERVING SUGGESTION **serve with steamed**
jasmine rice.

mains

97

satay beef and stir-fried vegetables with rice

SERVES 4
PREPARATION TIME 20 MINUTES
COOKING TIME 20 MINUTES
PER SERVING 14G FAT;
570 CALORIES (2387KJ)

1 litre (4 cups) water
1 cup (200g) basmati rice
1 teaspoon peanut oil
500g lean beef topside, sliced thinly
1 large brown onion (200g), sliced thinly
1 clove garlic, crushed
2 teaspoons grated fresh ginger
2 red thai chillies, deseeded and chopped finely
1 medium red pepper (200g), chopped coarsely
1 medium green pepper (200g), chopped coarsely
100g button mushrooms, halved
225g can bamboo shoots, drained
1 teaspoon curry powder
2 teaspoons cornflour
$1/2$ cup (125ml) chicken stock
$1/4$ cup (65g) low-fat smooth peanut butter
2 tablespoons oyster sauce
1 tablespoon unsalted, roasted, coarsely chopped peanuts

1 Bring the water to a boil in large saucepan; stir in rice. Boil, uncovered, about 15 minutes or until rice is just tender. Drain, rinse under hot water; drain rice again, cover to keep warm.
2 Meanwhile, heat oil in wok or large non-stick frying pan; stir-fry beef, in batches, until browned all over.
3 Reheat meat juices in same wok; stir-fry onion and garlic until onion softens. Add ginger, chilli, peppers, mushrooms, bamboo shoots and curry powder; stir-fry until vegetables are just tender.
4 Blend cornflour with stock in small jug; pour into wok, stir to combine with vegetable mixture. Return beef to wok with peanut butter and oyster sauce; bring to a boil, stirring, until sauce boils and thickens slightly and beef is cooked as desired. Stir in peanuts; serve with rice.

TIP you can use sliced lamb fillets or sliced chicken thigh fillets instead of the beef, if you prefer.

crisp beef with baby bok choy and noodles

SERVES 4
PREPARATION TIME 15 MINUTES
COOKING TIME 15 MINUTES
PER SERVING 47.3G FAT;
861 CALORIES (3605KJ)

2 tablespoons cornflour
$^1/_2$ teaspoon bicarbonate of soda
600g beef rump steak, cut into thin strips
$^2/_3$ cup (160ml) peanut oil
2 tablespoons sweet chilli sauce
$^1/_4$ cup (60ml) sweet soy sauce
1 tablespoon light soy sauce
2 teaspoons sesame oil
1 clove garlic, crushed
2 spring onions, chopped finely
400g fresh thin egg noodles
200g shiitake mushrooms, quartered
$^1/_2$ small chinese cabbage (400g), shredded coarsely
300g baby bok choy, sliced thinly lengthways

1 Combine cornflour and soda in large bowl. Add beef; toss to coat all over, shaking off excess.
2 Heat a third of the peanut oil in wok or large frying pan; stir-fry about a third of the beef until crisp. Drain on absorbent paper, then cover to keep warm; repeat with remaining peanut oil and beef.
3 Combine sauces, sesame oil, garlic and onion in small bowl.
4 Place noodles in large heatproof bowl, cover with boiling water; separate with fork, drain.
5 Reheat same cleaned wok; stir-fry mushrooms about 2 minutes or until just tender. Add cabbage and bok choy; stir-fry 1 minute. Add sauce mixture, noodles and beef; stir-fry until heated through.

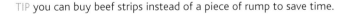

TIP you can buy beef strips instead of a piece of rump to save time.

mains

101

mashed potatoes three ways

Each of these three different mash recipes takes 15 minutes to prepare and about 15 minutes to cook. The key to perfect mash is to work quickly so that the hot potato is mashed and combined with other warmed ingredients then served immediately.

creamed spinach mash

SERVES 4
PER SERVING 37.2G FAT;
484 CALORIES (2025KJ)

1kg desiree potatoes, chopped coarsely
20g butter
1 clove garlic, crushed
125g baby spinach leaves
300ml cream, warmed

1 Boil, steam or microwave potatoes until tender; drain.
2 Meanwhile, melt butter in large frying pan; cook garlic and spinach, stirring, until garlic is fragrant and spinach wilted. Blend or process spinach mixture with half of the cream until mixture is pureed.
3 Place hot potatoes in large bowl; mash until smooth, then stir in spinach puree and remaining cream.

feta and black olive mash

SERVES 4
PER SERVING 22.1G FAT;
408 CALORIES (1709KJ)

1kg desiree potatoes, chopped coarsely
2 tablespoons olive oil
$^2/_3$ cup (160ml) buttermilk, warmed
200g feta cheese, chopped finely
100g pitted black olives, sliced thinly

1 Boil, steam or microwave potatoes until tender; drain.
2 Place hot potatoes in large bowl; add half of the oil, mash until smooth, then stir in remaining ingredients. Drizzle with remaining oil.

wasabi mash

SERVES 4
PER SERVING 17.8G FAT;
302 CALORIES (1266KJ)

1kg desiree potatoes, chopped coarsely
$^2/_3$ cup (160ml) cream, warmed
1 teaspoon wasabi paste

1 Boil, steam or microwave potatoes until tender; drain.
2 Place hot potatoes in large bowl; mash until smooth, then stir in remaining ingredients.

tiramisu

Low-fat ricotta turns this wicked dessert into a deliciously light treat that can be enjoyed by all.

SERVES 12
PREPARATION TIME 20 MINUTES
(PLUS REFRIGERATION TIME)
COOKING TIME 25 MINUTES
PER SERVING 4.1G FAT;
189 CALORIES (791KJ)

3 eggs
$1/2$ cup (110g) caster sugar
$1/4$ cup (40g) wholemeal self-raising flour
$1/4$ cup (35g) white self-raising flour
$1/4$ cup (35g) cornflour
1 teaspoon gelatine
1 tablespoon cold water
$1^1/2$ cups (300g) low-fat ricotta cheese
$1/4$ cup (60ml) skimmed milk
$1/4$ cup (55g) caster sugar, extra
2 tablespoons instant coffee powder
2 tablespoons boiling water
$1/3$ cup (80ml) skimmed milk, extra
$1/2$ cup (125ml) coffee-flavoured liqueur
10g dark chocolate, grated finely

1 Preheat oven to moderate. Grease and line base of a 22cm springform tin.

2 Using electric mixer, beat eggs in small bowl until thick and creamy. Gradually add the $1/2$ cup of sugar, beating until it dissolves. Fold triple-sifted flours into egg mixture until just combined. Spread into prepared tin.

3 Bake, uncovered, in moderate oven about 25 minutes. Turn onto wire rack to cool.

4 Meanwhile, sprinkle gelatine over the cold water in small heatproof jug; place jug in small pan of simmering water, stir until gelatine dissolves. Cool for 5 minutes.

5 Blend or process ricotta, $1/4$ cup of milk and the extra sugar until smooth. With motor operating, add gelatine mixture; process until combined. Dissolve coffee in the boiling water in small bowl; add the extra milk and liqueur.

6 Cut cake in half horizontally. Return one cake half to same springform tin; brush half of the coffee mixture over cake; top with half of the ricotta mixture. Repeat with remaining cake half, coffee mixture and ricotta mixture.

7 Refrigerate tiramisu, covered, for at least 3 hours. Sprinkle top with grated chocolate just before serving.

desserts

apple bread pudding

SERVES 6
PREPARATION TIME 20 MINUTES
COOKING TIME 1 HOUR 10 MINUTES
(PLUS STANDING TIME)
PER SERVING 3.6G FAT;
167 CALORIES (698KJ)

2 medium apples (300g)
2 tablespoons brown sugar
1 tablespoon water
2^1/$_2$ cups (625ml) skimmed milk
1 vanilla pod, halved lengthways
4 slices thick fruit bread
3 eggs
^{1}/$_2$ teaspoon ground cinnamon
^{1}/$_4$ teaspoon ground nutmeg

1 Peel, core and quarter apples; cut each quarter into 3mm slices. Dissolve brown sugar in the water in medium frying pan over low heat, add apples; simmer, uncovered, about 5 minutes or until tender, stirring occasionally.
2 Preheat oven to moderately slow. Grease a deep 1.5-litre (6 cup) ovenproof dish.
3 Combine milk and vanilla pod in medium saucepan; bring to a boil. Remove from heat; stand, covered, for 5 minutes. Discard vanilla pod.
4 Meanwhile, cut bread slices into quarters. Arrange bread and apple in alternate layers in prepared dish.
5 Whisk eggs, cinnamon and nutmeg in medium bowl. Gradually whisk hot milk mixture into egg mixture. Pour egg mixture carefully over bread and apple. Place dish in large baking dish; add enough boiling water to baking dish to come halfway up side of pudding dish.
6 Bake, uncovered, in moderately slow oven about 1 hour or until set. Serve with low-fat ice-cream or cream, if desired.

breakfasts

chocolate ricotta tart

Chocolate chips are great to use when baking because they hold their shape and add an explosive chocolatey crunch

SERVES 8
PREPARATION TIME 15 MINUTES
(PLUS REFRIGERATION TIME)
COOKING TIME 35 MINUTES
PER SERVING 6.5G FAT;
169 CALORIES (706KJ)

$1/4$ cup (35g) white self-raising flour
$1/4$ cup (40g) wholemeal self-raising flour
2 tablespoons caster sugar
2 teaspoons cocoa powder
30g low-fat dairy-free spread
2 teaspoons water
1 egg yolk

RICOTTA FILLING
150g low-fat ricotta cheese
1 egg
1 egg yolk
$1/4$ cup (70g) low-fat plain yogurt
$1/4$ cup (55g) caster sugar
2 teaspoons plain white flour
2 tablespoons dark chocolate chips
2 teaspoons coffee-flavoured liqueur

1 Grease an 18cm-round loose-based flan tin.
2 Process flours, sugar, sifted cocoa and spread until crumbly; add the water and egg yolk, process until ingredients just cling together. Knead dough gently on lightly floured surface until smooth, cover; refrigerate 30 minutes.
3 Preheat oven to moderately hot.
4 Press dough into prepared tin; cover with baking parchment large enough to extend 5cm over edge, fill with dried beans or rice. Bake, on a baking tray, in a moderately hot oven for 10 minutes; remove beans and paper. Bake for a further 5 minutes or until pastry is lightly browned; cool.
5 Reduce temperature to moderate. Pour ricotta filling into tin; bake, uncovered, in a moderate oven about 20 minutes. Cool; refrigerate until firm.

RICOTTA FILLING using electric mixer, beat ricotta, egg, egg yolk, yogurt, sugar and flour in medium bowl until smooth. Stir in chocolate chips and liqueur.

chocolate mousse

The word mousse is a French description for froth or foam, a look usually achieved by lots of calorie-laden whipped cream. Here, we've used low-fat fromage frais for equally delicious results, but without the excess fat and energy.

SERVES 8
PREPARATION TIME 10 MINUTES
(PLUS REFRIGERATION TIME)
PER SERVING 8.09G FAT;
228 CALORIES (955KJ)

1 tablespoon instant coffee powder
1 tablespoon cocoa powder
2 teaspoons hot water
160g dark chocolate, melted
3 cups (800g) vanilla low-fat fromage frais
50g dark chocolate, grated, extra

1 Dissolve coffee and cocoa in the water in medium bowl. Stir in melted chocolate and fromage frais; beat with electric mixer on medium speed about 3 minutes or until mixture is smooth.
2 Divide mixture evenly among eight $^1/_2$-cup (125ml) serving glasses. Cover; refrigerate overnight.
3 Serve chocolate mousse sprinkled with the grated chocolate.

TIP Try to find a fromage frais containing less than 0.5g fat per 100g; substitute a low-fat vanilla yogurt if you cannot find it, but be aware that the fat and calorie count will rise slightly if the fat content is higher.

SERVING SUGGESTION serve mousse topped with fresh berries – raspberries team especially well with chocolate.

chocolate brownie

MAKES 16
PREPARATION TIME **15 MINUTES** COOKING TIME **25 MINUTES**
PER BROWNIE **3.8G FAT; 73 CALORIES (303KJ)**

2 eggs
$^1/_3$ cup (75g) firmly packed brown sugar
2 teaspoons instant coffee powder
2 tablespoons cocoa powder
1 tablespoon water
1 tablespoon olive oil
40g low-fat dairy-free spread, melted
$^1/_4$ cup (40g) wholemeal self-raising flour
$^1/_4$ cup (45g) dark chocolate chips
1 teaspoon cocoa powder, extra
2 teaspoons icing sugar mixture

1 Preheat oven to moderate. Grease and
line a deep 19cm-square baking tin.
2 Using electric mixer, beat eggs and
sugar in small bowl until thick and creamy.
Transfer to medium bowl.
3 Meanwhile, blend coffee and cocoa
with the water and oil in small bowl
until smooth. Stir in spread. Fold cocoa
mixture into egg mixture; fold in flour and
chocolate chips. Pour mixture into
prepared pan.
4 Bake, uncovered, in a moderate oven
for about 25 minutes or until brownie is
firm to the touch. Stand 30 minutes; turn
onto wire rack. Serve brownie dusted with
sifted combined extra cocoa and icing
sugar mixture, and low-fat ice-cream,
if desired.

pears poached in cranberry syrup

SERVES 4
PREPARATION TIME 5 MINUTES
(PLUS STANDING TIME)
COOKING TIME 45 MINUTES
PER SERVING 0.2G FAT; 281 CALORIES (1178KJ)

*If beurre bosc pears are unavailable,
use packham or williams pears.*

3 cups (750ml) cranberry juice
^{2}/$_3$ cup (160ml) dry white wine
2 cardamom pods, bruised
^{1}/$_2$ vanilla pod, halved lengthways
4 medium beurre bosc pears (920g)

1 Combine juice, wine, cardamom and
vanilla pod in large saucepan.
2 Add peeled pears to pan; bring to a boil.
Reduce heat; simmer, covered, for about
25 minutes or until tender. Cool pears
in syrup.
3 Remove pears from syrup; strain syrup
into a medium heatproof bowl. Return
2 cups of the strained syrup to the same
pan (discard remaining syrup); bring to a
boil. Boil, uncovered, about 15 minutes or
until syrup is reduced by half. Serve pears,
hot or cold, with syrup.

TIP pears can be poached a day ahead; reduce the syrup just
before serving.

breakfasts

lime cheesecake

The long refrigeration times required for this cheesecake are a bonus when entertaining ... make it ahead so you're free to devote all your attention to the rest of the menu on the day of the meal.

SERVES 8
PREPARATION TIME 30 MINUTES
(PLUS REFRIGERATION TIME)
COOKING TIME 10 MINUTES
PER SERVING 6.7G FAT;
185 CALORIES (773KJ)

80g plain biscuits
40g low-fat dairy-free spread, melted
2 teaspoons gelatine
1 tablespoon water
$^1/_3$ cup (80ml) lime juice
$^2/_3$ cup (150g) sugar
$^1/_2$ cup (100g) low-fat ricotta cheese
100g pack low-fat cream cheese
2 teaspoons finely grated lime rind
3 egg whites

1 Grease an 18cm springform tin; line base with baking parchment.
2 Blend or process biscuits and dairy-free spread until mixture resembles fine breadcrumbs. Using one hand, press biscuit mixture evenly over base of prepared tin. Refrigerate until firm.
3 Sprinkle gelatine over the water in heatproof jug; stand jug in medium saucepan of simmering water. Stir until gelatine dissolves; reserve mixture.
4 Combine juice and sugar in small saucepan. Stir over heat, without boiling, until sugar dissolves; bring to a boil. Reduce heat; simmer for 1 minute.
5 Meanwhile, beat cheeses and rind in medium bowl with electric mixer until mixture is smooth.
6 Beat egg whites in small bowl with electric mixer until soft peaks form; with motor operating, gradually add hot sugar syrup. Whisk slightly warm gelatine mixture and egg white mixture into cheese mixture; pour mixture into prepared pan. Cover; refrigerate about 2 hours or until set.

SERVING SUGGESTION
pipe whipped light cream on cheesecake and decorate with thin lime wedges just before serving.

TIP if you don't own a citrus zester, grate only the green outer rind of a lime on the tiniest holes of a four-sided grater. Avoid grating any of the bitter white pith.

black forest parfaits

SERVES 6
PREPARATION TIME 30 MINUTES
(PLUS REFRIGERATION TIME)
PER SERVING 3.2G FAT;
305 CALORIES (1277KJ)

2 x 85g packets cherry flavour jelly crystals
6 mini jam rolls (150g), chopped coarsely
$^1/_4$ cup (60ml) sweet sherry
425g can pitted black cherries, drained
$1^1/_2$ cups (375ml) low-fat vanilla custard
3 x 20g low-fat chocolate bars, sliced thinly

1 Make jelly according to directions on packet; place in large jug. Refrigerate about 1 hour or until jelly is almost set.
2 Meanwhile, combine jam rolls and sherry in small bowl. Reserve half of the jam roll mixture; cover until required. Divide remaining half among 6 x $1^1/_3$-cup (330ml) serving glasses.
3 Pour half of the jelly mixture evenly over jam roll mixture in glasses; sprinkle with half of the cherries. Refrigerate 5 minutes. Continue layering with remaining jam roll mixture, then all of the custard, the remaining jelly and, finally, the remaining cherries. Cover parfaits; refrigerate overnight.
4 Serve parfaits sprinkled evenly with chocolate.

SERVING SUGGESTION
serve topped with whipped light cream.

breakfasts

melon granita trio

SERVES 8
PREPARATION TIME 45 MINUTES
(PLUS FREEZING TIME)
COOKING TIME 10 MINUTES
PER SERVING 0.6G FAT;
234 CALORIES (979KJ)

3 cups (750ml) water
1 1/2 cups (330g) sugar
800g cantaloupe melon, seeded, peeled and
coarsely chopped
800g honeydew melon, seeded, peeled and
coarsely chopped
800g watermelon, seeded, peeled and coarsely
chopped

1 Combine the water and sugar in medium saucepan. Stir over heat, without boiling, until sugar dissolves; bring to a boil. Reduce heat; simmer, uncovered, without stirring, about 2 minutes or until syrup thickens slightly.

2 Blend or process the cantaloupe until almost smooth; push through sieve into a shallow cake tin. Combine with a third of the sugar syrup. Repeat process with the honeydew and half of the remaining syrup in a separate cake tin, then with the watermelon and remaining syrup in another cake tin.

3 Cover each tin with aluminium foil; freeze about 3 hours or until granita mixtures are just set.

4 Keeping granita mixtures separate, scrape into bowls, then beat each with electric mixer until smooth. Return each to their respective tins, cover with foil; freeze overnight or until each granita sets firmly.

5 Serve granita, layered in alternate scoops, in individual glasses.

SERVING SUGGESTION
granitas are delicious on a hot day served on top of bowls of seasonal fruit salad.

desserts

honey buttermilk ice-cream with fresh fruit salsa

Buttermilk is a tangy dairy product made in a similar way to yogurt. It has a fat content of 1.8g per 100ml. We used low-fat evaporated milk with a fat count of 1.6g per 100ml.

SERVES 6 (APPROXIMATELY 2 LITRES ICE-CREAM)
PREPARATION TIME 30 MINUTES (PLUS FREEZING TIME)
COOKING TIME 15 MINUTES
PER SERVING 7G FAT; 341 CALORIES (1426KJ)

2 teaspoons gelatine
$1/4$ cup (60ml) water
$1^1/2$ cups (375ml) low-fat evaporated milk
$1/2$ cup (175g) honey
$1^1/2$ cups (375ml) buttermilk

FRUIT SALSA
1 small pineapple (800g), chopped coarsely
1 large mango (600g), chopped coarsely
3 medium kiwi fruit (255g), chopped coarsely
250g strawberries, chopped coarsely

1 Sprinkle gelatine over the water in a small heatproof jug; stand jug in pan of simmering water. Stir until gelatine dissolves; cool.
2 Meanwhile, place evaporated milk in a medium saucepan; bring to a boil. Remove from heat; stir in gelatine mixture and honey. Transfer to a medium bowl; cool.
3 Beat buttermilk in a small bowl with electric mixer until frothy.
4 Beat evaporated milk mixture with electric mixer until light and frothy. With motor operating, gradually pour in buttermilk; beat until combined.
5 Pour into 2-litre (8 cup) metal container. Cover with aluminium foil; freeze about 3 hours or until just set.
6 Beat ice-cream with electric mixer until smooth. Re-cover with foil; freeze overnight or until set. Serve ice-cream with fruit salsa.

FRUIT SALSA Combine fruit in medium bowl.

TIP ice-cream can also be made in an ice-cream maker.

breakfasts

121

vanilla pod ice-cream with espresso sauce

SERVES 4
PREPARATION TIME 10 MINUTES
(PLUS FREEZING TIME)
COOKING TIME 15 MINUTES
(PLUS STANDING TIME)
PER SERVING 7G FAT;
231 CALORIES (965KJ)

1 vanilla pod
1 cup (250ml) low-fat evaporated milk
$^1/_3$ cup (80ml) low-fat cream
2 egg yolks
$^1/_2$ cup (110g) caster sugar
$^1/_2$ cup (125ml) boiling water
1 tablespoon ground espresso coffee beans

1 Split vanilla pod lengthways; scrape seeds into a small saucepan. Add vanilla pod, evaporated milk and cream; bring to a boil. Remove pan from heat, cover; stand 20 minutes. Discard vanilla pod.
2 Meanwhile, using electric mixer, beat egg yolks and sugar in small bowl until thick and creamy; gradually stir in vanilla mixture.
3 Return mixture to same pan; cook, stirring, over low heat, about 15 minutes or until mixture thickens slightly (do not allow to boil).
4 Strain ice-cream mixture into 20cm x 30cm shallow rectangular baking pan, cover surface with foil; cool to room temperature. Freeze until almost set.
5 Place ice-cream in large bowl; chop coarsely. Using electric mixer, beat ice-cream until smooth. Pour into 14cm x 21cm loaf pan, cover; freeze until ice-cream is firm.
6 Just before serving, combine the water and coffee in coffee plunger; stand 2 minutes before plunging. Cool 5 minutes before serving over ice-cream.

desserts

mini lemon yogurt cakes with syrup

MAKES 30
PREPARATION TIME 10 MINUTES
COOKING TIME 15 MINUTES
PER CAKE 0.6G FAT;
29 CALORIES (121KJ)

The combination of lemon, yogurt and poppy seeds lends an eastern Mediterranean accent to these morsels.

$^1/_3$ cup (50g) self-raising flour
$^1/_4$ cup (55g) caster sugar
1$^1/_2$ tablespoons cornflour
$^1/_4$ teaspoon bicarbonate of soda
1 teaspoon poppy seeds
1 egg yolk
$^1/_4$ cup (70g) plain yogurt
$^1/_2$ teaspoon finely grated lemon rind
1 teaspoon lemon juice
10g butter, melted

LEMON SYRUP
1 medium lemon (140g)
$^1/_4$ cup (55g) sugar
$^1/_4$ cup (60ml) water

1 Preheat oven to moderate.
2 Sift flour, sugar, cornflour and soda into small bowl; stir in poppy seeds, egg yolk, yogurt, rind, juice and butter.
3 Drop rounded teaspoons of mixture into mini cake cases on a baking tray. Bake in moderate oven 10 minutes. Drizzle or brush hot lemon syrup over the hot cakes.

LEMON SYRUP using a vegetable peeler, remove rind from lemon; shred peel finely. Juice the peeled lemon; place 2 teaspoons of the juice (reserve remainder for another use) in small saucepan with shredded rind, sugar and the water. Stir over heat, without boiling, until sugar dissolves. Boil, uncovered, without stirring, for about 5 minutes or until mixture thickens slightly; transfer to small heatproof jug.

TIP use a vegetable peeler to remove the lemon rind before you juice the citrus.

conversion charts

MEASURES

The cup and spoon measurements used in this book are metric: one measuring cup holds approximately 250ml; one metric tablespoon holds 20ml; one metric teaspoon holds 5ml.

All cup and spoon measurements are level. The most accurate way of measuring dry ingredients is to weigh them. When measuring liquids, use a clear glass or plastic jug with metric markings.

We use large eggs with an average weight of 60g.

WARNING This book contains recipes for dishes made with raw or lightly cooked eggs. These should be avoided by vulnerable people such as pregnant and nursing mothers, invalids, the elderly, babies and young children.

DRY MEASURES

metric	imperial
15g	$^1/_2$oz
30g	1oz
60g	2oz
90g	3oz
125g	4oz ($^1/_4$lb)
155g	5oz
185g	6oz
220g	7oz
250g	8oz ($^1/_2$lb)
280g	9oz
315g	10oz
345g	11oz
375g	12oz ($^3/_4$lb)
410g	13oz
440g	14oz
470g	15oz
500g	16oz (1lb)
750g	24oz (1$^1/_2$lb)
1kg	32oz (2lb)

LIQUID MEASURES

metric	imperial
30ml	1 fl oz
60ml	2 fl oz
100ml	3 fl oz
125ml	4 fl oz
150ml	5 fl oz ($^1/_4$ pint/1 gill)
190ml	6 fl oz
250ml	8 fl oz
300ml	10 fl oz ($^1/_2$ pt)
500ml	16 fl oz
600ml	20 fl oz (1 pint)
1000ml (1 litre)	1$^3/_4$ pints

LENGTH MEASURES

metric	imperial
3mm	$^1/_8$in
6mm	$^1/_4$in
1cm	$^1/_2$in
2cm	$^3/_4$in
2.5cm	1in
5cm	2in
6cm	2$^1/_2$in
8cm	3in
10cm	4in
13cm	5in
15cm	6in
18cm	7in
20cm	8in
23cm	9in
25cm	10in
28cm	11in
30cm	12in (1ft)

OVEN TEMPERATURES

These oven temperatures are only a guide for conventional ovens. For fan-assisted ovens, check the manufacturer's manual.

	°C (Celcius)	°F (Fahrenheit)	gas mark
Very low	120	250	$^1/_2$
Low	150	275-300	1-2
Moderately low	170	325	3
Moderate	180	350-375	4-5
Moderately hot	200	400	6
Hot	220	425-450	7-8
Very hot	240	475	9

index